If you were a

Prefix

by Marcie Aboff
illustrated by Sara Gray

PICTURE WINDOW BOOKS
Minneapolis, Minnesota

prefix a letter or group of letters placed before a word to change its meaning

Editor: Christianne Jones
Designer: Hilary Wacholz
Page Production: Melissa Kes
Art Director: Nathan Gassman
The illustrations in this book were created with acrylics.

Picture Window Books
1710 Roe Crest Drive
North Mankato, MN 56003
www.capstonepub.com

Copyright © 2009 by Picture Window Books, a Capstone imprint. All rights reserved. No part of this book may be reproduced without written permission from the publisher. The publisher takes no responsibility for the use of any of the materials or methods described in this book, nor for the products thereof.

Library of Congress Cataloging-in-Publication Data
Aboff, Marcie.
If you were a prefix / by Marcie Aboff ; illustrated by Sara Gray.
p. cm. — (Word fun)
Includes index.
ISBN-13: 978-1-4048-4773-6 (library binding)
ISBN-13: 978-1-4048-4777-4 (paperback)
ISBN-13: 978-1-4795-8363-8 (saddlestitch)
1. English language—Suffixes and prefixes—
Juvenile literature. I. Gray, Sara, ill. II. Title.
PE1175.A23 2008
428.1—dc22 D08006347

Printed in the United States 5605

Looking for prefixes?

Watch for the underlined letters throughout the book.

Special thanks to our advisers for their expertise:

Rosemary G. Palmer, Ph.D., Department of Literacy
College of Education, Boise State University

Terry Flaherty, Ph.D., Professor of English
Minnesota State University, Mankato

If you were a prefix ...

... you would come first!

Prefixes can make a regular school a preschool,
change angles, to triangles,
and make lucky unlucky.

If you were a prefix, you would be a letter or group of letters placed before a word to change its meaning.

The colorful caterpillar <u>trans</u>formed into a <u>multi</u>colored butterfly.

If you were the prefix "re," you could do things over again.

During the rematch, the giraffe rebounded the ball and dribbled down the path.

The monkey had to
replay the phone
message about replacing
the missing bananas.

If you were the prefix "co," you could help do an important job.

The copilot helped the pilot fly the airplane.

The co-captain helped the captain steer the ship.

If you were the prefix "tele," you could talk to, see, and watch things far away.

The owl called the eagle on the telephone.

The robin looked for the eagle with a telescope.

The birds watched their favorite show on television!

If you were a prefix, you could give a word added meaning.

The jaguar looked like a star driving his ordinary car.

The jaguar looked like a
superstar driving his
extraordinary car.

If you were a prefix, you could change the same word in different ways.

You could make a cycle a unicycle, a bicycle, or a tricycle.

If you were a prefix, you could change a word to mean its opposite.
The happy rabbit jumped out of the hole, and his friends appeared.

The unhappy rabbit climbed into the hole, and his friends disappeared.

If you were a prefix, you could be yourself. The prefix *pre* means "before." The word *fix* means "to place." *Prefix* means "to place before."

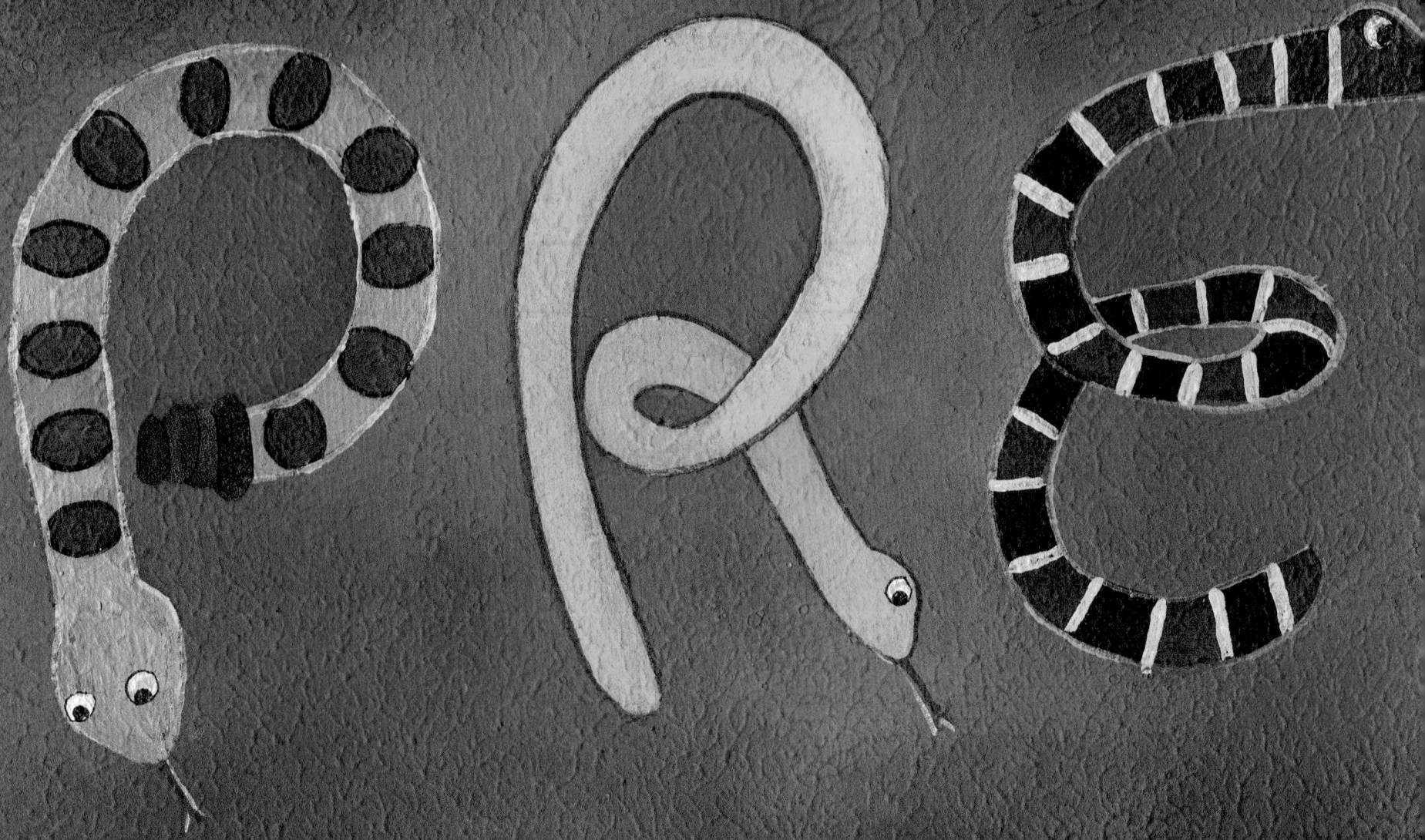

You would always come first ...
Prefix
FINISH
... if you were a prefix.

FUN WITH SUFFIXES

Cut out 20 pieces of paper and mix them up. On each piece of paper, write one of the suffixes or root words from below. Mix them up. Then, see if you can match them and put the words back together. Next, make your own list and have a friend match the words. You can even time each other and see who can match the words the fastest.

brave ly
move ment
dark ness
interest ing
lemon ade

neighbor hood
wood en
free dom
taste ful
use less

Glossary

past tense—a verb showing something that happened in the past
plural—more than one
present tense—a verb showing something happening in the present moment
root—the basic meaning of the word
suffix—a letter or group of letters added to the end of a word to change its meaning

To Learn More

More Books to Read

Draze, Dianne. *Red Hot Root Words.* Austin, Tex.: Dandy Lion Publications, 2003.

Heinrichs, Ann. *Prefixes and Suffixes.* Chanhassen, Minn.: Child's World, 2006.

LoGiudice, Carolyn, and Kate LaQuay. *Spotlight on Vocabulary, Prefixes and Suffixes.* East Moline, Ill.: LinguiSystems, Inc., 2005.

On the Web

FactHound offers a safe, fun way to find Web sites related to topics in this book. All of the sites on FactHound have been researched by our staff.

1. Visit *www.facthound.com*
2. Type in this special code: 140484774X
3. Click on the FETCH IT button.

Your trusty FactHound will fetch the best sites for you!

Index

changing "y" to "i," 21
past tense, 18-19
plural, 10
present tense, 18-19
root word, 20
suffix "d" or "ed," 18-19
suffix definition, 6
suffix "er," 8-9
suffix "est," 16-17
suffix "ful," 12-13
suffix "less," 14-15
suffix "s" or "es," 10-11

Look for all of the books in the Word Fun series:

If You Were a Compound Word
If You Were a Conjunction
If You Were a Contraction
If You Were a Homonym or a Homophone
If You Were a Noun
If You Were a Palindrome
If You Were a Prefix
If You Were a Preposition
If You Were a Pronoun
If You Were a Suffix
If You Were a Synonym
If You Were a Verb
If You Were Alliteration
If You Were an Adjective
If You Were an Adverb
If You Were an Antonym
If You Were an Interjection
If You Were Onomatopoeia